GUILDFORD

10
TOWN AND
COUNTRY

RAMBLES

Written and Illustrated
by Chris Howkins

Mapwork
Darren Hemsley

WRITTEN AND ILLUSTRATED
Chris Howkins

MAPWORK
Darren Hemsley

COPYRIGHT
Chris Howkins 1991 ©

PUBLISHED
Chris Howkins,
70, Grange Road,
New Haw,
WEYBRIDGE,
Surrey, KT15 3RH.

PRINTED
Unwin Brothers Limited,
The Gresham Press,
OLD WOKING,
Surrey, England.
GU22 9LH.

ISBN 0 9509105 8 9

CONTENTS

INTRODUCTION

Guildford is beautifully situated in the centre of West Surrey where the River Wey has cut through the line of the North Downs, known on the west side as The Hog's Back. It is a landscape of wooded hills separated out by vales of fields and trees and more woods. The High Street itself looks across to fields and trees on the hillside beyond the river - staunchly defended lest a sea of suburban rooftops make this their high tide mark.

Thankfully there are so many villages around Guildford to accommodate people that the town itself is not engulfed in suburbia. The building of a new A3 has even improved districts like Burpham - a few years ago the walk back from there into town centre was a nightmare of traffic but now the old A3 has become the A25 it is quite pleasant at off-peak times.

The historic town centre has been savaged not salvaged. The Victorians considered seriously knocking down the castle and replacing it with a bandstand. They didn't but much else has gone over the last hundred years. What is left is a collection of fine buildings. What has gone is the mass of lesser buildings to illustrate the social setting of those monuments.

Guildford is not an industrial town today yet it certainly had an industrial heart along the riverside, with breweries, mills, iron works, timber yards etc. All that industrial heritage has been swept ruthlessly away. The opportunity to create a beautiful riverside to set off the famous High Street was lost too, given over to ugly traffic schemes. Only a couple of old warehouses and the Rodborough Buildings survived. The latter, built in 1901

4

survived. The latter, built in 1901, is 'probably the oldest surviving purpose-built multi-storey car factory in Britain," and that too has only recently survived demolition by the skin of its teeth. Guildford is now trying to make the best of what is left. Anyone who is interested in modern architecture will find plenty to go and look at and much of it is worth the look. Thus another layer of interest is being added to this ancient town, which, even in Saxon times, was sufficiently important to be minting the coinage for a time.

THIS BOOK aims to help visitors find the best, without wasting too much time trudging up and down the hillside. Obviously it has not been possible to include everything of note nor to relate fully why those included are considered worthy of note.

Then there is the beautiful countryside all around, from the Downs to the riverside, with such beauty spots as Newlands Corner, St.Martha's and the Silent Pool. These are the places visitors are told regularly that they 'must' see and so these have been chosen for inclusion rather than some of the lesser known places. Anyone with the opportunity can ramble round Guildford for years and not exhaust the interest.

As per the rest of the series the emphasis is upon shorter rambles to allow time to stop and look, see and enjoy. Some of the rambles can be joined together to please those who like to clock up a good few miles and guidance for that is given next.

5

The illustrations
have been included to
encourage as much
looking as walking;
about a third of them
have not been published
before.

Wey Navigation material
has been in print before and
is issued again in this form to
please those readers of The Towpath
Book who have requested something
smaller to take out with them.

Further Information is available
from the Information Centre (High
Street), the Museum (Quarry Street)
and the Library (North Street).
The main buildings issue their
own guide books.

Easy wheeling
Guidance is given in the text
as to suitability for wheelchairs and
pushchairs by mentioning steps, stiles,
steep hills etc. Compared with the other
books in this series wheelchair users come off poorly,
with only parts of the town and parts of the Shalford
and Merrow village rambles being readily accessible.

THANKS are due to the many people who, over the years,
have shared their knowledge which has made this book
possible; then to Darren Hemsley who scouted the routes,
checked the directions, mapped them, and helped put the
final manuscript together, and finally, to Sue Harvey
for checking the typscript.

WARNING – The inclusion of a path in this book
is no indication that it is a public right of
way.

MAPS are **NOT** drawn to scale.

JOINING THE RAMBLES TOGETHER

The first two rambles, around the town link up at the top of the High Street. Ramble 2 takes in part of Chertsey Street which can be followed out to Stoke for the last ramble in the book. Alternatively, from the High Street ramble 7 can be added on.

For a complete circuit of the town link up the first three rambles, and add ramble 4 for good measure although you may prefer to walk back from St. Catherine's along the main road rather than repeat part of The Mount.

Ramble 8 to St.Martha's includes the first part of ramble 1 and more could be added from the town rambles. Ramble 8 links up with ramble 9. There are paths from Newlands Corner to link up with ramble 7 but a good map is needed, unless the road is followed.

The towpath provides a valuable guide for linking the three upstream riverside rambles - 4,5 and 6, and also for downstream rambles - parts of ramble 3 and then 10.

Numbers as per Contents page

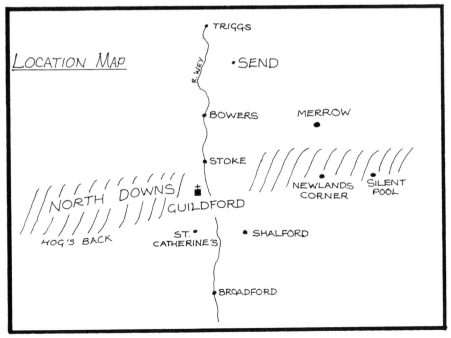

TOWN CENTRE
some of the main sites

START (S on map) at the
bottom of the High Street
or join route wherever
convenient.

WALK UP HIGH STREET.
FIRST RIGHT INTO
QUARRY STREET.

QUARRY STREET does not
climb the Downs but takes
an easy course to the side,
parallel to the river and thus
prompts suggestions that this
was the very first of Guildford's
streets, especially as it has along
it the town's oldest building –
St. Mary's Church.

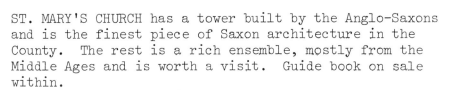

Tower of
St. Mary's
11th C. +

ST. MARY'S CHURCH has a tower built by the Anglo-Saxons
and is the finest piece of Saxon architecture in the
County. The rest is a rich ensemble, mostly from the
Middle Ages and is worth a visit. Guide book on sale
within.

ROSEMARY ALLEY descends as great flights of steps to
the river valley below. It is the last such alley in
Guildford and nowhere else in Surrey captures past times
in quite this way. The buildings that hem it in look
17th century but their internal structures are far older.

QUARRY STREET'S BUILDINGS on the left hand side are
following the course of the castle's outer wall. Here
you will find the HQ of the Surrey Archaeological Soc.,
the Guildford Muniment Room and GUILDFORD MUSEUM. The
oldest parts of their building were constructed between
1611 and 1630.

8

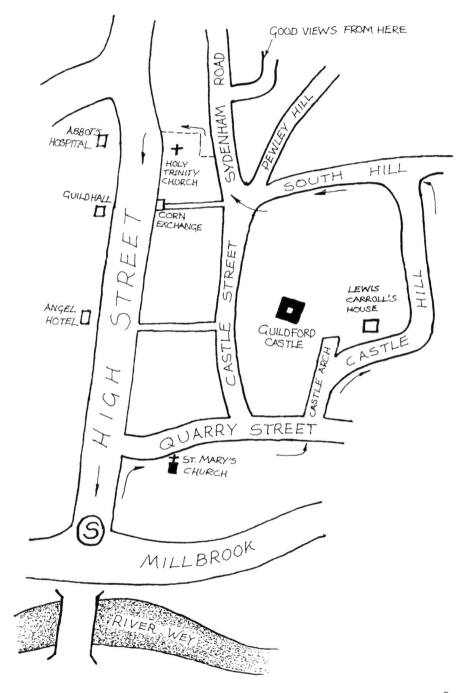

A FORMER DISPENSARY with
its plaque can be spotted
on the left. It was
rediscovered in 1987
when a Victorian frontage
was demolished to reveal
the 17th century building
behind. In 1859 it
became Guildford's first
public dispensary with
ten local doctors on
call and one resident
medical officer. Work
ceased here in 1866
when the first Royal
Surrey County Hospital
opened in Farnham Road.

NO 49, TRAYLENS BOOKSHOP
was built in 1760 for a
doctor but was taken over
in 1822 for housing the
Assize Court Judges on
circuit.

CASTLE ARCH, over a
road of that name, is
the only impressive
piece of outer castle
masonry to survive.
It is believed to be
the arch documented
as being designed
by John of Gloucester.
He was a prominent
stone mason in the
city of Gloucester
and was taken into
royal service and
rose to become
Master Mason of
The King's Works.

ROSEMARY ALLEY

From 1254-56 John of Gloucester was "in charge of
repairs to the hall and other parts of the royal
palace at Guildford, next to the castle, damaged
by fire, according to the king's personal instructions
by word of mouth." With such high office came "two
robes yearly, with furs of good squirrels" John also
managed to get the same for his wife,
Agnes, as well! At this time he was
giving "view and counsel" on the
building of the arch. He died a few
years later, in 1260. A sculpted
portrait head, high up in the north
transept of Westminster Abbey is
thought to be of this great mason.

TURN LEFT THROUGH CASTLE ARCH
AND PROCEED UP THE HILL.

More masonry from the castle site
can be seen from the public garden
on the right. Ahead, a gate leads
into more public gardens on the
left where there is more masonry
and views across to the keep on its
mound. Little is understood clearly about the exact
layout of the palace area cum castle but fresh work on
excavation began in 1990

AT THIS POINT EITHER EXPLORE THE CASTLE GROUNDS
UP TO THE TOP ENTRANCE OR ELSE FOLLOW THE ROAD
ROUND AS PER THE SKETCH MAP.

Following Castle Hill soon brings you into its dog-leg
and there on the left is THE CHESTNUTS built about 1861
and leased out to the Rev. Charles Dodgson in 1868.
This mathematics don at Christchurch, Oxford, wanted it
for his six unmarried sisters and here he used to come
to stay - of interest because he was "Lewis Carroll" of
Alice in Wonderland fame. From here he went to preach
in St.Mary's, to the theatre over the river (now part
of The Guildford School of Acting, and from here in

1898 he was taken
to The Mount
cemetery on the
opposite hillside,
having died on
14th January.
There is a display
relating to the
writer in Guildford
Museum, and a
commemorative
sculpture down on
the riverbank at Mill-
mead. For now, as you

pass by
The Chestnuts, notice the plaque on
the gatepier, decorated with his
characters.

Follow the hill on round for views
of Guildford few people bother to
come and find, or, cut back through
the castle grounds.

The palace and castle declined to the
point where they were of no further value to the Crown
and so James I sold them off in 1611. In 1885 they
were bought by Guildford Corporation and various ideas
were put forward, like replacing the keep with a bandstand. Fortunately the keep was retained and the land
opened as public gardens in 1888 to commemorate the
50th year of Victoria's reign. The keep, built c.1125,
is open during the summer and provides grand views of
the town from the top. It was never used defensively,
(it quickly surrendered during the troubles following
Magna Carta) but it was a favourite royal residence
until the 14th century.

MAKE YOUR WAY TO THE TOP ENTRANCE TO THE
CASTLE GROUNDS/JUNCTION WITH SOUTH HILL.

LOOK down the wall behind the grass
towards the keep and you will spot three
plaques by local artist Ann Garland depicting
historic scenes from Guildford's history.

TURN ROUND and look up at the end of the Tunsgate
building and there you will see another of her designs:
the great sundial showing Edward I and his queen,
Eleanor of Castile, who knew Guildford well. Of their
thirteen children their only surviving son was crowned
Edward II. The sundial was executed by Richard Quinnell
at Oxshott Road, Leatherhead. He is an important
figure in the modern revival of fine art metalsmithing.

If you need to shorten this ramble you can return to the
High Street by walking through Tunsgate, if not....

CONTINUE UP ALONG SYDENHAM ROAD TO THE MULTI-
STOREY CAR PARK AND AFTER IT TURN LEFT DOWN AN
ALLEY.

Before you do so, there is the option of walking on as
shown on the sketch map for a vantage point overlooking
the town.

13

WALK DOWN THE ALLEY TOWARDS HOLY TRINITY CHURCH AND FOLLOW THE DOG-LEG ROUND THE CHURCHYARD

You are plunged suddenly into an old part of Guildford and very attractive it is too. HOLY TRINITY CHURCH is the only large 18thC. church in Surrey although the east end is Victorian. It is built in very correct Palladian style and served as Guildford's first cathedral.

GEORGE ABBOT, ARCHBISHOP OF CANTERBURY, died in 1633 and was buried here in his home town. In 1640 was erected the monument to him, in the south transept, showing the primate on a heap of books with skulls and bones between to remind us how short will be our earthly life. As an artistic style it revived a medieval theme but was of short duration itself. The whole of the tomb is in a very conservative style; indeed the whole church is restrained.

THE WESTON CHAPEL survived the rebuilding and dates from the late medieval period. Sir Richard Weston held high offices for Henry VIII; his son, Francis, was knighted by the king and then executed for supposed adultery with Anne Boleyn; another Sir Richard was the agricultural pioneer and founder of the Wey Navigation.

SIR RICHARD ONSLOW has a monument here too. He was local Member of Parliament and Speaker in the House of Commons for thirty three years. The story of this great family can be explored further at Clandon Park.

LEAVE THE CHURCH AND CROSS THE HIGH STREET TO ABBOT'S HOSPITAL OPPOSITE

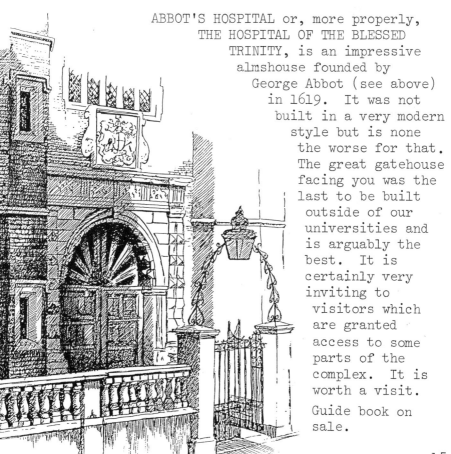

ABBOT'S HOSPITAL or, more properly, THE HOSPITAL OF THE BLESSED TRINITY, is an impressive almshouse founded by George Abbot (see above) in 1619. It was not built in a very modern style but is none the worse for that. The great gatehouse facing you was the last to be built outside of our universities and is arguably the best. It is certainly very inviting to visitors which are granted access to some parts of the complex. It is worth a visit.

Guide book on sale.

15

Notice the Royal Arms of
James I over the door.
When this Scottish king
took the English throne
the Royal Arms had to be
changed and so for the
first time the royal heraldry
of Scotland was marshalled
with that of England, hence
the red lion in the second
quarter and the unicorn as
one of the supporters. For
the first time too the harp
of Ireland appears in the third
quarter. The Royal Arms in this
form were used publicly for seventy
four years.

ON LEAVING GATEHOUSE TURN RIGHT TO WALK DOWN THE HIGH STREET TO THE STARTING POINT.

THE HIGH STREET has won wide acclaim for its scenic
qualities as it plunges steeply down to the river with
views across to green meadows on the Down beyond. The
surface, still cobbled with 'sets', also pleases many
people.

Now that traffic is restricted severely there is more
chance to view the buildings, many of which appear to
be newish but are hiding ancient structures. Among all
these are some of Guildford's prize possessions...

THE CORN EXCHANGE is the first to look for (left)
comprising a robust great Tuscan portico across the
side street at Tunsgate. It was built in 1818 by
Henry Garling at a cost of just under £5,000, raised
by public subscription. How grand it must have looked
amid the smaller scale buildings of that time! It
housed also the Assize Court and on those occasions the
unsold corn had to be shovelled out, but eventually,
after 700 years, Guildford lost the right to hold the
Assizes and they went to Kingston. The Corn Exchange
became redundant and for many years the arguments raged

as to what should
be done with the
building. It
narrowly escaped
destruction and
was eventually
only destroyed
in part so as
to retain the
main portico in
its present form and use.

On the RIGHT look for a fine old house with much
decoration, which was originally CHILD HOUSE, named
after a Mayor of Guildford, but now known as GUILDFORD
HOUSE. Dating from 1660 it is the best of the older
surviving houses and the carvings are worth a careful
look (binoculars a great asset).

Next on the right look for Guildford's most famous
building - the GUILDHALL - not that you can miss it
with John Aylwards grand clock dated 1683 projecting
out over the street. The whole building is wonderful
because it breaks all the architectural rules and then
proves itself right for doing so.

TOURIST INFORMATION OFFICE on the left is housed in a
medieval undercroft and so is worth visiting for that.

THE ANGEL on the right, the sole survivor of the town's
famous coaching inns, has a dignified stuccoed street
facade and then rambles back into a confusion of
timber framing at least as old as the 17th century.

TOWN CENTRE : Upper Town
Distance : 1⅖ miles

START (S ON MAP) AT HOLY TRINITY STEPS AT THE
TOP OF THE HIGH STREET, OUTSIDE ABBOT'S
HOSPITAL.

This ramble can be added on to the first one
if time and energy permit. It has been split
for the benefit of explorers with wheelchairs
or push-chairs which will be able to follow
this route. The first ramble has steps and
is very steep in parts.

More main sites are located along this ramble
but you will also discover some of
the lesser buildings of note.
Sadly there are few groups,
of merit, of lesser status
left in Guildford to show
the full range of its
social development and
so this corner becomes
more precious every
year.

FROM TRINITY STEPS
CROSS THE HIGH STREET
TO THE LEFT OF ABBOT'S
HOSPITAL AND TURN DOWN
JEFFRIES PASSAGE.

Guildford has several
narrow shopping streets
but this is the closest
of all. Today it
leads to North Street
but formerly to the
town ditch of waste
disposal!

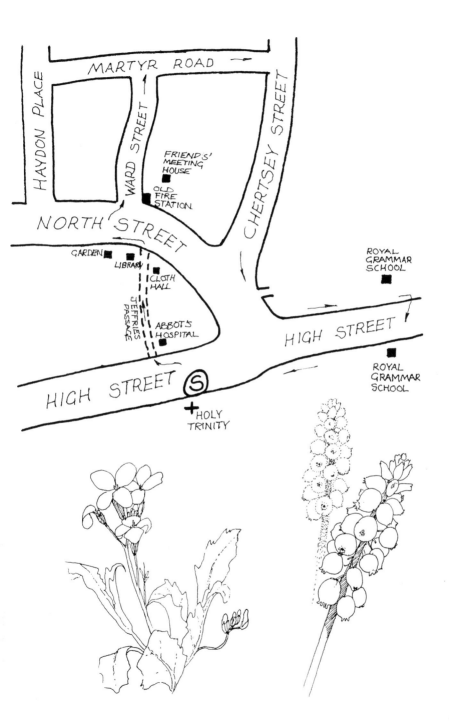

MARTYR ROAD

HAYDON PLACE

WARD STREET

CHERTSEY STREET

FRIENDS' MEETING HOUSE

OLD FIRE STATION

NORTH STREET

GARDEN

LIBRARY

CLOTH HALL

JEFFRIES PASSAGE

ABBOT'S HOSPITAL

ROYAL GRAMMAR SCHOOL

HIGH STREET

HIGH STREET

S

HOLY TRINITY

ROYAL GRAMMAR SCHOOL

19

You step out of the Passage into the top part of North
Street which is the only part worth exploring. It is
comparatively new, having been the town ditch before.
At the end of the week it is busy with street traders.

THE PUBLIC LIBRARY is on your left, first opened in 1961
and one of the best buildings of that date in Guildford.
On the top floor is the LOCAL STUDIES LIBRARY where you
can get additional information about the town. From the
window on the stairs you get a good view into the backs
of the Abbot's Hospital.

Next to the Library is QUAKERS' ACRE, developed by the
Society of Friends when their meetings became legal
in the late 17thC. The plot was given to the
town in 1927 and is now used
as a public garden.

The present Quaker meeting house is across the road but first, as you look over, note a smart little brick building rising to a central clock turret. This grand little building now houses public toilets but was once the home of the Guildford fire engine! The fire station was built by a fascinating man called Henry Peak – one of those Victorian gentlemen who, with no formal education or training, rose from nothing to be a leading townsman. He was nineteen when he arrived in Guildford and set about making himself an architect until he became the first Borough Surveyor – a job he held for twenty eight years during which he contributed much to Guildford, from saving the castle to starting the first major new housing areas. He crowned it all off by serving as mayor.

CROSS OVER TO WARD STREET

Before going down Ward Street, look back at Abbot's Hospital to see the fine Jacobean architecture again. See also how well the modern additions have been made. Of particular interest is the large building on the right hand side, terminating in a Victorian tower that butts into the pavement. The older part behind dates from 1619 as a cloth hall which was George Abbot's attempt to revive the failing woollen cloth industry for which Guildford had been famous for hundreds of years. Abbot himself was the son of a cloth worker; he was a success but his cloth hall was not.

ENTER WARD STREET

On the corner is the GUILDFORD INSTITUTE, working well in the townscape as it sweeps the eye down the street long and slightly concave facade.

21

The Guildford Institute was founded in 1834 but many internal wrangles meant that this building was not erected until 1892, by which time much of the enthusiasm for Gothic Revival architecture was over. The neighbouring buildings here show how dull it had become. Thus for the Institute a much more domestic style was chosen and it works well in the townscape.

Through this gateway opposite is the FRIENDS' MEETING HOUSE. We don't know exactly when the Quakers began meeting in Guildford because at first they were illegal assemblies but this building was erected in 1805 in sober red brick with round-headed windows in keeping with Quaker beliefs. This area – Guildford, Godalming, Worplesdon etc, was one of the early centres of the Quakers in Surrey, attracting leading figures such as William Penn and the Founder of the movement, George Fox.

TURN RIGHT UP MARTYR ROAD

There's a whole range of architecture here. On your right is a wonderful great terrace, incorporating the local flint. It is not often we find a terrace of this date in a town built with flint: it was more fashionable and more economic to use mass produced brick.

Over the road is the SURREY ADVERTISER building: a scarce 1930s building (1936), distinctive with its rounded corners. The surfaces were not originally so bland but covered with tiles. Alas these became unsafe and have had to be removed.

Enjoy the variety, including some of
the modern work, but before turning
right at the top deviate to the
left just far enough to pass the
first modern block. Beside it
you will get a surprise. When
the site was being redeveloped
an old timber-framed building came
to light and as you see, it was saved
and restored. Its setting, when first
built was in a landscape of fields, before Guildford
spread this far beyond the ditch (North Street).

TURN RIGHT UP CHERTSEY STREET

TURN LEFT UP NORTH STREET

TURN LEFT ALONG THE UPPER
HIGH STREET

Collared Dove

Finally on this ramble comes the
famous Royal Grammar School. On this
left hand side are the modern buildings
but before you turn away look at the name board and note
the Royal Arms. They are not those currently in use but
those used by Edward VI (reigned 1547-1553) during whose
reign provision for education was greatly increased and
included Guildford. The Arms are not what the text books
would lead us to expect: the first quarter (France Modern)
ought to have three fleur-de-lys as first established by
Henry IV about 1400. The harp of Ireland came into
general use with James I. The supporters, a gold lion
and a red dragon are standard Tudor, introduced by Henry
VII. He and his son had alternatives but Edward VI kept
to the lion and the dragon while his successor, Mary,
introduced variety again.

CROSS THE ROAD TO THE OLD SCHOOL BUILDINGS

Here you see a fine Tudor building of stone. They are
a rarity in Surrey. This is the finest public building,
with Loseley nearby as a grand private house and a small

23

house stands near Haslemere station. The Royal Grammar
School was founded in 1509 although the buildings we
see today were begun mid century and earned their royal
charter on 27th January 1553. In those days this was
in countryside on the edge of the town and as you look
towards town centre you are looking across the cricket
pitch used by the boys in about 1550. That is quoted
often as the first written record of the game but back
in the 28th year of the reign of Edward I there is a
reference to the younger Edward: "ad ludendum ad creag'
et alios ludos" where creag is an abbreviation for
creagit which was their spelling of cricket.
As Edward I spent part of his youth at
Guildford Palace maybe it was here
that he learned the game.

RETURN TO START

G.Hawkins 1985/6
The Angel, Guildford.

TOWN CENTRE : Dapdune Wharf
The Cathedral
The Mount

Distance : 2¾ miles approx.

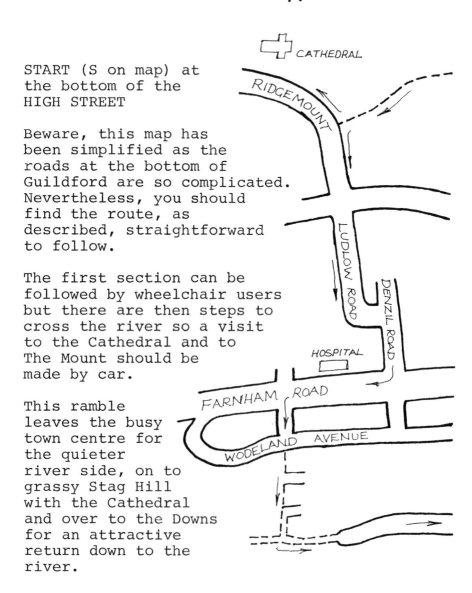

CATHEDRAL

RIDGEMOUNT

LUDLOW ROAD

DENZIL ROAD

HOSPITAL

FARNHAM ROAD

WODELAND AVENUE

START (S on map) at
the bottom of the
HIGH STREET

Beware, this map has
been simplified as the
roads at the bottom of
Guildford are so complicated.
Nevertheless, you should
find the route, as
described, straightforward
to follow.

The first section can be
followed by wheelchair users
but there are then steps to
cross the river so a visit
to the Cathedral and to
The Mount should be
made by car.

This ramble
leaves the busy
town centre for
the quieter
river side, on to
grassy Stag Hill
with the Cathedral
and over to the Downs
for an attractive
return down to the
river.

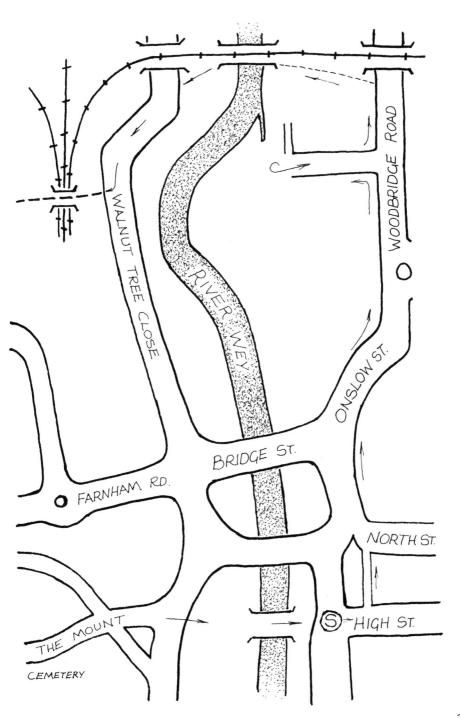

WALNUT TREE CLOSE

WOODBRIDGE ROAD

RIVER WEY

ONSLOW ST.

BRIDGE ST.

FARNHAM RD.

NORTH ST.

THE MOUNT

CEMETERY

HIGH ST.

27

START as though to walk up the HIGH STREET but take the first turning left which is a narrow shopping arcade for pedestrians only. It will take you through to the bottom of NORTH STREET.

CONTINUE AHEAD, crossing North Street and following the buildings round until you can get over on to the LEFT hand pavement by way of one of the pedestrian crossings.

FOLLOW this out, past the multi-storey car park and the Law Courts so that you are walking out of town along WOODBRIDGE ROAD.

TURN LEFT down WHARF ROAD beside the cricket ground.

TURN RIGHT at the bottom.

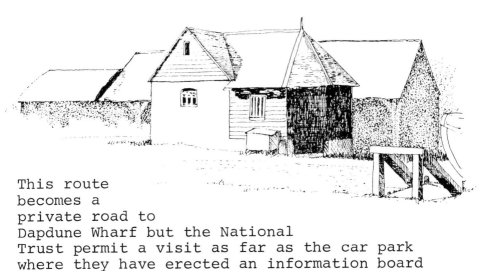

This route
becomes a
private road to
Dapdune Wharf but the National
Trust permit a visit as far as the car park
where they have erected an information board
explaining what can be seen.

This site is being developed as a Heritage Centre by
the National Trust to record the days (1653-1958) when
the river was used by commercial barge traffic. This
wharf opened soon after the waterway and has become the
last to survive in Guildford. Until recently it was
derelict and overgrown as in the sketch (bottom left)
made in 1982. Now you will find that all has been
cleared and being restored. At the time of writing, the
riverbank itself was being restored to safeguard the
original railway and crane on its brink. When all has
been made safe it is planned to admit the public but
until then please stay in the car park.

The nearest building, illustrated above, was a stable
for the wharf horse and the end furthest away was the
blacksmith's workshop where he made the massive iron
nails used in building barges here. The other side of
his workshop had facilities for steaming the oak planks
until they were supple enough to bend round to make the
prow of a barge.

Beyond this building was found the original dry dock,
now restored and with it the two capstans. With four
men on each it was possible to wind a barge right out
of the river and that is exactly what the National Trust

29

did in 1989 when this barge was rescued from the Thames
mud at Leigh-on-Sea and brought back to the place where
it had been built in 1936. The National Trust hope to
house museum displays within it soon.

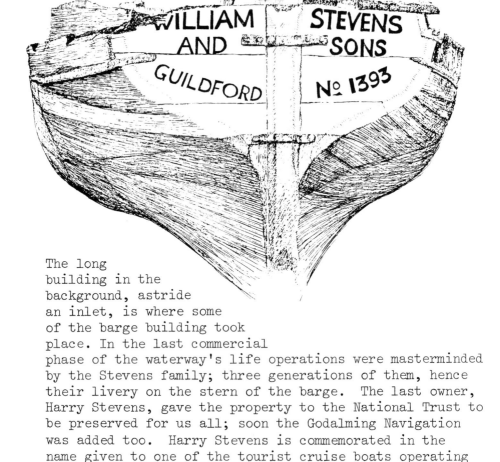

The long
building in the
background, astride
an inlet, is where some
of the barge building took
place. In the last commercial
phase of the waterway's life operations were masterminded
by the Stevens family; three generations of them, hence
their livery on the stern of the barge. The last owner,
Harry Stevens, gave the property to the National Trust to
be preserved for us all; soon the Godalming Navigation
was added too. Harry Stevens is commemorated in the
name given to one of the tourist cruise boats operating
from Guildford Boat House behind Millmead car park.

RETRACE your route out of Dapdune Wharf, up
Wharf Road and then TURN LEFT along WOODBRIDGE
ROAD as far as the railway bridge.

TURN LEFT down footpath immediately before
railway and so up over the bridge.

The footbridge on the railway viaduct affords good views including one down onto Dapdune Wharf. The viaduct itself was built in 1885 by the London and South Western Railway to carry their line from Guildford to Hampton Court. It's a fine brick structure - the best around Guildford but there are also fine ones in the Mole Valley at Leatherhead, Norbury Park, etc.

DESCENDING FROM THE BRIDGE - KEEP LEFT to walk up the road, to continue the route as mapped.

Anyone wishing to return to the start at this time will find the walk up the towpath direct and more interesting than the other options.

A short diversion up the first part of the towpath and back affords views across the river to Dapdune Wharf. The housing can be seen well, as per the sketch below.

The larger dwelling on the left once housed the master builder of the barges. The cottages on the right were once used as a store for gunpowder. This was an important cargo on the Wey Navigation from the Chilworth works further up the valley.

The Heritage Centre is still
being developed and so the
view may have changed by
the time you see it. The
sketch below was made
in 1982 before the
undergrowth was
cleared.

FROM THE VIADUCT walk left up the road that
cuts through the RIVERSIDE BUSINESS PARK.
This is only a short section through commercial premises
but how different they are from what is likely to spring
to mind at the mention of commercial premises. Whether
you like modern buildings or not these are better surely
that what would have been done to the site in the 1960s!

LOOK FOR A FOOTPATH UP AN ACCESS ROAD ON THE
RIGHT, (It is signposted "to the University"
on the left). FOLLOW this to the RAILWAY BRIDGE.

The view left includes Guildford Railway Station. This
was intially on a spur from Woking from where the first
train had departed at 7.30 am on May 5th 1845. Free
beer was given to all the workmen to celebrate.

The trains you see today are very different from those
first planned which "comprised engines and coaches using
flangeless wooden wheels to be run on flat wooden track
with additional guide wheels pressing at angles to the
sides and the tops of the rails." This system had been
patented by a Mr.Prosser in 1844, the year the Guildford
Junction Company was authorised to build the line. It
would not be compatible with the system used by the
London and South Western Railway at Woking and so the
company bought the new line and operated conventional
trains on it. Prosser got £2,000 compensation.

AT THE END OF THE RAILWAY BRIDGE
KEEP LEFT TAKING THE PATH THROUGH
THE TREES. Do not go on to the
University site.

TURN RIGHT when you reach the
road. Soon there will be an
entrance to the Cathedral on
your right; or rather, to the
hill. A long flight of steps
leads to the top and you will
find the entrance at the west
end.

It was May 17th 1961 that Her Majesty
Queen Elizabeth II came here for the
service of consecration of the new
Cathedral, performed by its first
bishop, Rt. Rev. George Reindorp who
had himself only been enthroned the
month before, at the former Cathedral
of the Holy Trinity at the top of the
High Street; the first enthronement
of a bishop ever to be televised in
this country.

When the idea of Guildford becoming
a Cathedral town was finally accepted
there much heated controversy as to
where the Cathedral should be – use
Holy Trinity, build afresh on Stoke
Park and so on. Lord Onslow brought
things to a head by giving six acres
of his land on the top of this hill,
Stag Hill, with the option of buying
more land if needed. That plan was
obviously fulfilled but not with
ease – it was too far from the town,
it was too separate from the town,
the geology was wrong, and so on.
That was in 1928. The Depression
followed but despite all the
difficulties Guildford had its

fine new Cathedral. It is a fine building, despite all the adverse criticisms thrown at it. By the time it was completed architecture had become thoroughly 'modern' and compared with new Cathedrals like Coventry and Liverpool this one seemed a very poor thing. People forgot that the competition to find a design was won by Sir Edward Maufe back in 1932 when it was much more difficult to nudge people into accepting newer trends in architecture.

He reduced the principles of Gothic Revival architecture to a minimum and thereby re-expressed them in a new and dignified way. Thus the building does look like a Cathedral and it does look Anglican (compare the Roman Catholic church of St. Michael, Ashford, by Sir Giles Gilbert Scott, begun 1928).

It gives a grand impression of size as you walk around to the west front, especially as the summit of the hill is left so bald. Beside you rise great walls of brick, lovely soft coloured brick, appropriate for a non-stone county like Surrey. It's easy to miss the finer details of sculpture such as the attenuated figures by Allan Collins, three of which are sketched here. Note also the metal castings on the doors, by Vernon Hill.

The great wooden cross at the east end was erected in 1933 to mark the site. It is of teak not oak.

To step inside is to find a scene
that will be familiar to Cathedral
explorers, sometimes described as
Curvilinear Gothic, but do not
anticipate architectural details
such as capitals, pronounced rib
vaulting and bosses. All such
features have been designed away
to leave pale cool simplicity.
Its impressiveness is subtle
rather than immediate.

Detailed guide books are of course
available for visitors.

**On leaving the Cathedral
RETRACE your route back
down the steps on the
south side and turn left
back along the road.**

**Instead of turning back on
to the footpath, keep on the
road. Look across the roofs
and you will see a large red
brick Victorian building.
Head straight for that.**

The route now skirts the N.E. edge
of Onslow Village created by the
Onslow Village Association which
was founded in 1920. Ten weeks
later and the first foundations
were being laid, on 1st May. It
drew inspiration from the Garden
City Movement and in particular
from the Hampstead Garden Suburb
project since one of the key figures
at Guildford had worked on the
Hampstead development. Thus the
area on your right comprises human
scale housing respecting the contours

Guildford Cathedral
2.6.85
Sketched from 'The Oval'
Onslow Village

of the land,
providing gardens
with hedges and other
subtle details to create personal
space and a sense of community. The little factories
and other places of work in the original concept did
not arise; more homes instead.

On approaching the big red brick building follow the road to skirt round the left side to the main Farnham Road and TURN RIGHT to walk in front of what now becomes apparent as a hospital.

 This opened as the Royal Surrey County Hospital in 1862 - one of many great Victorian institutions in the County as the population grew together with a sense of public duty to provide all manner of social services. Guildford did not get as many as places like Woking and Redhill because it was that little further out of London, from whence many originated. Also, it was later getting the railway.

Another example stands next door - the Hillier Alms-houses, which have an inscription telling us that the charity was founded and endowed for seven women by Elizabeth Hillier in 1800. Her brother, Nathaniel Hillier, enlarged it for eight women in 1812. It was originally in the Curtain Road, Shoreditch but, like the Rowland Hill Almshouses at Ashford, the charity moved out. Nathaniel Hillier lived in Guildford at Stoke Park.

CROSS THE FARNHAM ROAD.
TURN RIGHT AND THEN LEFT UP ANNANDALE ROAD

AHEAD A FOOTPATH CUTS STRAIGHT UP THE SIDE OF THE DOWNS. TAKE THAT TO THE TOP.

TURN LEFT ALONG THE TRACKWAY (If you take a detour right you soon come to Henley Fort, the most western of a line of London defences against possible invasion (c.1897-1905).

You have now climbed from the new Farnham Road that developed in the 19th century to the old Farnham Road which it replaced. The old road is very ancient and mentioned in a charter of 1189. It became a turnpike in 1759. Now it is a peaceful route back to Guildford, with good viewpoints over the town and surrounding countryside.

As you descend the hill you will
pass the Mount Cemetery, started
in 1856. Turn through the gate
to the chapel and on the far side
next to the path under the conifer
is the grave of the Rev. Charles
Lutwidge Dodgson (Lewis Carroll)
who died in Guildford of the 'flu'
on January 14th 1898. Others of
his family are buried here too.

Directly below the Beech tree is the
white headstone of local artist
Ann Garland who designed the
Tunsgate sundial and the town's
history plaques.

The tower at the far end of the
cemetery was erected in 1839 by
Charles Booker as a 'prospect tower'
from which to enjoy the view. It
made a good observation post in
World War II.

The ramble continues down the hill
through some of Guildford's finer
old houses. Of these many appear
to be Georgian but this 18th century
appearance often conceals far older
structures behind. Some go back another
couple of centuries.

It is difficult to believe this steep narrow
hill was once the main carriageway to Farnham.
It does still afford an impressive approach to
the town centre as the High Street comes into view
running up the opposite hillside from the river. If
this side is in shadow and the other side is sunlit then
it is especially memorable.

Look ahead and you will see the way over the main road
to St.Nicolas's Church and the Town Bridge beside it
and so to the starting place for this ramble.

MILLMEAD AND ST. CATHERINE'S

Distance : 2½ miles approx.

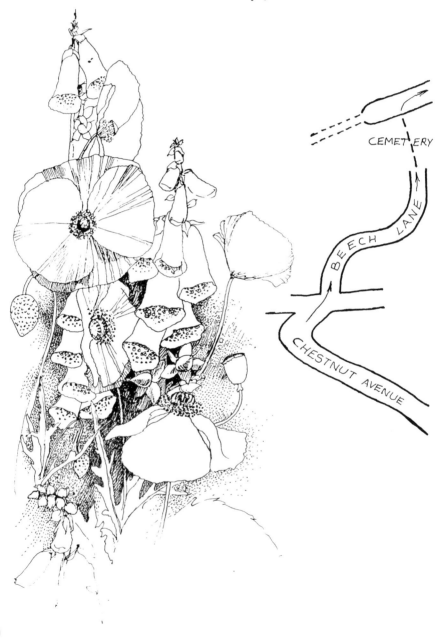

CEMETERY

BEECH LANE

CHESTNUT AVENUE

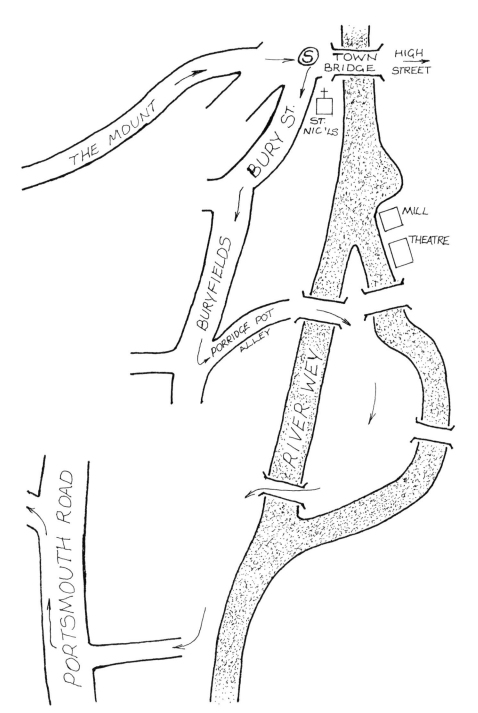

THE MOUNT

S

TOWN BRIDGE

HIGH STREET

BURY ST.

ST. NIC'LS

MILL

THEATRE

BURYFIELDS

PORRIDGE POT ALLEY

RIVER WEY

PORTSMOUTH ROAD

41

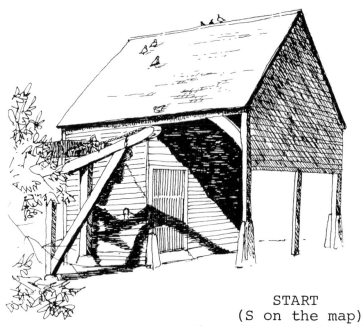

START
(S on the map)
at the bottom of the High
Street and use the underpass to
reach the TOWN BRIDGE (see plaque).

LOOKING DOWNSTREAM note the building illustrated above
which can be approached by a walkway. It is one of the
nation's very few machines listed as an Ancient Monument
for this is a crane. It dates from the second half of
the 17th century and was operated by no more than two
men (despite what some books say) trundling round the
giant (18 ft diameter) treadwheel inside the building.
It is an impressive reminder of the days when the river
was used as a commercial waterway, with many tons of
goods to shift in and out of barges all along the river
here; this was a former meal wharf. The crane itself
will lift only about one ton (despite what some books
say!) and was still in use in the 1920s. The only other
examples in Britain are at Harwich and Kings Lynn.

On the wall beside the building are plaques illustrating
the history of Guildford.

The River Wey opened to commercial traffic as far as
the bridge in 1653; as you look upstream you view the
Godalming Navigation extension which opened in 1764.

THE CHURCH on the right is
dedicated to St.Nicolas,
retaining the medieval
way of spelling the name.
The church retains also
the 15thC. Loseley
Chapel but otherwise
dates from 1875 (the
work of S.S.Teulon and
Ewan Christian). At the
time of the rebuild the
new vicar fell while
inspecting the foundations
and subsequently died.
He was Dr. John Monsell
the hymn writer. Another
incumbent here of note was
Nicholas Andrews, back in Puritan

times, who was ejected and chained aboard a prison ship
"to hasten the end of his life" - because he did what
the law said he should! In the narthex of the church is
a memorial to Caleb Lovejoy whose work comes next.....

ROUND THE CHURCH INTO BURY STREET

Walking along the relative quietness of this street note
the Caleb Lovejoy Almshouses on the left, built from the
income of his property in London. There wasn't much of
an income! That's why these were not built until 1838
when Lovejoy had died in 1676 although the money did
have to be divided between more than one scheme. The
almshouses look especially attractive from the top of the
rise ahead.

House No.15 on the corner was built during Caleb's life
and has managed to keep one of the four Dutch gables
that are such a beautiful feature of the architecture of
that time. In the late 18thC. the front was remodelled
and given its Tuscan porch. Despite changes and time it
still makes a distinctive feature in the townscaping of
the corner. There are other distinctive houses in this
small section of the town making detours worthwhile but
for the moment...

BEAR LEFT ALONG BURYFIELDS

BURYFIELDS is another quiet street, not unpleasant to walk along, with two more of Guildford's undervalued buildings. Firstly, on the right, "The Court" - a three-sided range of housing with mature garden in the centre. It looks 1920s but was built in 1902 and is thus "considered to be of outstanding architectural importance because of its advanced design." It is the work of a local architect, H. Thackeray Turner, who provided the district with a range of fine buildings but who has sadly been overshadowed by other famous local architects like Sir Edwin Lutyens.

Enjoy this building and then move on to the corner of the street ahead where you will find another of Turner's works. You are unlikely to recognize it - it is so very different yet only seven years older. It is the cottage built of local sandstone. Note the proportions and masses and the eye for details and you'll begin to see what makes it so masterly.

Look up the hill beside the cottage (Millmead Terrace) to the great red brick building at the top. What a contrast! With the cottage nothing was overstated but on this building (architect uncertain) everything masons could achieve with stone was copied here by bricklayers: stepped gables, ball finials, concave niches, fluted pilasters, balustrading, and florid swags to hold the date. It's now part of Guildford School of Acting but as can be seen up in a gable it was built in 1887 as a Workingmen's Club. It was part of the social provision made by the parish of St.Nicolas which had a really flourishing spiritual life (detailed in its guide book). The illustration opposite is only part of the building.

TURN LEFT DOWN PORRIDGE POT ALLEY

This walkway leads back to the riverside and the ramble continues over the footbridge ahead. Keep this in mind because on a sunny day there will be great temptation to divert to the left for a few moments to explore this cul-de-sac, known as Millmead. It will be difficult to imagine this lined with wharves with a great timber yard and an iron works but that is how it once was.

44

Diverting up Millmead will bring you back to the Town
Bridge (good view of it with civic heraldry in the
quarterfoils) and just before it, the popular green with
a sculpture to commemorate Lewis Carroll's association
with the town. Over the river is the Yvonne Arnaud
Theatre (her ashes were scattered on St.Martha's Hill -
see separate ramble). The theatre was designed in the
early 1960s when its modernity caused quite an outcry
in some quarters. How acceptable it looks today!

Beside it swirls the ancient mill pool with mill beyond.
There have always been mills along here. William the
Conqueror had one here. Today's dates from 1770 with
a mid 19thC. extension. It last milled flour in 1894.

Continuing the ramble...

CROSS THE FOOTBRIDGE onto the land between the two waterways. TURN RIGHT.

The ramble turns right but a quick return route to the start is straight ahead over the lock and through the footway to the main road and turn left.

THE LOCK is the first on the Godalming Navigation; there are only three more on the four mile journey up to Godalming. The towpath can be walked all the way.

FOLLOW THE PATH UPSTREAM AND BEAR RIGHT TO CROSS A FOOTBRIDGE AND CONTINUE AHEAD ALONG THE TOWPATH.

This scene soon comes into view although probably not with water on both sides of the bank. The field beyond is used to collect flood water should it threaten Guildford. On the distant hill can be seen the ruins of St.Catherine's Chapel.

FOLLOW THE TOW
PATH ROUND TO
ST CATHERINE'S
HILL where a
lane comes in
from the right.

TURN RIGHT
and follow
the lane out
to the main
Portsmouth Road.

Deviate up one of the
paths to the ruined
chapel on top of St.
Catherine's Hill. It was
built in 1317 and must have
been very striking when the rubble walls were newly
plastered over, the windows were complete with tracery
and the corner turret and the pinnacles along the sides
were all rising high, and with the sun catching a fresh
coat of limewash.

The views are worth the scramble up the hill (site of a
former fair). The river cum Navigation cuts in deep
below but a little way further upstream, at St.Catherine's
lock, they separate or rather rejoin, after the river has
wound its way through the meadows and trees to the edge of
the village of Shalford - green copper spire in the trees
marks the church.

OPTIONS : EITHER continue with this ramble, OR,
if you have been attracted by the view from the
top of St.Catherine's, extend your route as per
the next ramble.

AT THE MAIN PORTSMOUTH ROAD TURN RIGHT

Shortly, on the right, is the entrance to 'The Valley'
(illustrated right) which is a 'pretty' Surrey-Victorian
development of 1881 and a good example of its type. The
main road can be unpleasantly busy so...

CROSS THE ROAD AND TAKE CHESTNUT AVENUE

48

This is a
quieter route
if you do not
mind the hills.
If time is short
follow the main road
straight back into
Guildford.

BEAR RIGHT AT THE
END OF CHESTNUT AVE.

CROSS OVER INTO BEECH LANE

FOLLOW BEECH LANE THROUGH TO THE CEMETERY

OUT THE FAR SIDE OF THE CEMETERY AND TURN
RIGHT DOWN THE MOUNT TO THE STARTING POINT.
A few details about the cemetery and The Mount were
given at the end of the last ramble.

ST. CATHERINE'S TO BROADFORD
Distance : 2 miles approx.

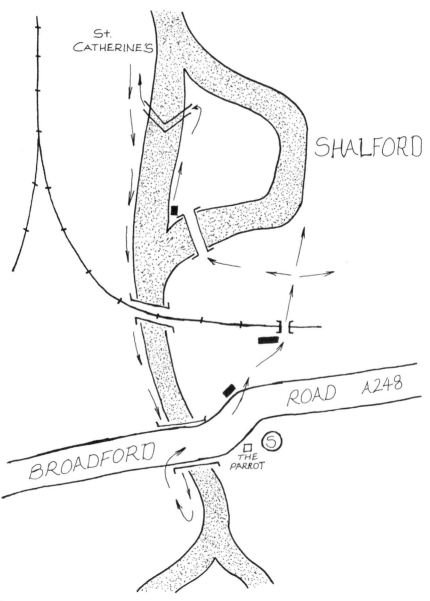

St.
CATHERINE'S

SHALFORD

ROAD   A248

BROADFORD

THE
PARROT   S

Looking downstream from St. Catherine's Lock to the ruined chapel on the skyline.

START
EITHER at the Parrot Inn on the A248 as per the directions here given, OR, join the circuit at St.Catherine's Lock by walking down from St.Catherine's Hill as an extension of the previous ramble.

The Parrot Inn can be reached by car by taking the A281 Horsham Road out of Guildford and turning right onto the A248 at Shalford Common or by taking the A3100 Godalming Road out of Guildford and turning left onto the A248 at Peasmarsh.

The beginning of this ramble is the same as for the next and so the two can be joined up for a longer walk.

This ramble is one of simple pleasures - walking down the towpath through a landscape of fields and trees and distant hills. The path can be soft underfoot in winter and is often decidedly wet on either side so dogs and little children can get very muddy!!

CROSS the road from The Parrot.
Take the rough track diagonally
across the common to the right
hand end of the distant terrace.

One of Shalford's ponds can be found at the left end of
the terrace; a pleasing spot to deviate to for a few
moments. The black waterbirds with white beaks are
coots, (above) while ones with red beaks are moorhens.

From the right hand end of the terrace follow
the track round the fronts of the cottages
and at the end spot a small brick bridge
ahead, by which you cross the railway.

Continue ahead.

On the left of this country path through the
trees you will find a stile which you cross.
The view from here, down into the valley bottom with
the river meandering through is especially attractive.

CROSS the stile and descend to the planks
across the wetlands. PROCEED to the river
bank and CONTINUE upstream.

You will arrive at a weir known as Riff-Raffs (can't
find out why - does any reader know?) where the River
Wey continues its journey out through the meadows to
Shalford where it loses about 6 million gallons into
the domestic supply system, while the rest of the water
continues off to the right as the Godalming Navigation
heading for Guildford.

CROSS the weir and skirt round the cottage
to continue along the bank of the Navigation.

This is another attractive
spot. The lock cottage
was built in 1909 for
£239. The walk down to
the lock is not very far
but is a wonderful open
place on a good day and
just as atmospheric when
the rain beats across.

CROSS the Navigation at the lock and TURN LEFT
to follow the towpath upstream.

The overflow loop around the lock is not part of the
original Navigation construction but was added in the
1930s as part of the River Wey Improvement Scheme.

Enjoy the walk up to Broadford Bridge and the cottage
scene shown below. People who knew this area a few
years ago will be pleased to know that the factory with
the tall chimney at Broadford has been swept away and
the view improved. The replacement building is a
good example of its kind and the grounds are well looked
after.

As the name suggests, this was once a ford in the Wey
and remained so after the Navigation came into use. It
must have been a very deep ford to let the barges
through and this caused problems. In 1769 the owner,

John Sparkes, had its safety improved and was so pleased with the result that he gave each of the workmen a shilling for a drink. In 1793 the first bridge was built. The present bridge is the lowest on the water-way and causes panic on many a boat!

Before crossing the bridge, rambles may like to walk a little further upstream to view the scene illustrated above.

This is the Gun's Mouth (again nobody seems to know the origin of the name) which is the entrance to the Wey & Arun Junction Canal - opened 1816, closed 1871 - which linked London with the South Coast without having to send vessels round the enemy-ridden coast. The more efficient railways put it out of use.

This part of the waterway has been improved by the National Trust who now own the meadows behind aswell so this should stay an attractive and historic spot.

RETURN TO THE BRIDGE

Over the river on your right was Stonebridge Wharf,
once very busy on this junction of the two waterways.
In part, it handled a specialised cargo, namely the
gunpowder produced at the nearby Chilworth works. The
building illustrated below was formerly used for storing
it ready for loading. Being raised on straddle stones
the building kept drier than might otherwise have been
the case.

TURN RIGHT TO CROSS THE BRIDGE

**FOLLOW the road round the bends and the
starting point is once again on your right.**
This is a dangerous set of bends so keep dogs and young
children under control.

SHALFORD
A Village Ramble
Distance : 1 ¾ miles

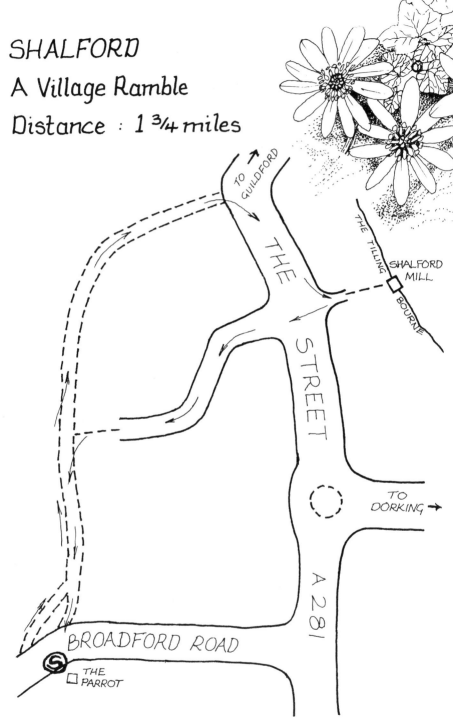

TO GUILDFORD

THE STREET

THE TILLING

SHALFORD MILL

BOURNE

TO DORKING

A 281

BROADFORD ROAD

THE PARROT

START at the Parrot inn
on the A248. To reach it
take the A281 Horsham road
out of Guildford and turn
right onto the A248 after
the village, or, take the
A3100 Godalming road out of
Guildford and turn left onto
the A248 at Peasmarsh.

Shalford is an attractive village but
suffers rather badly from the main road
through the street and across the green.
This ramble is chosen to avoid the traffic
as much as possible.

CROSS the road from The Parrot.
Take the rough track diagonally
across the common to the right
hand end of the next row of
cottages and follow track round.

There are groups of workers' cottages dotted
around the greens making an uncommon feature.
Note here the creamy blocks used with red brick
quoins in some of the cottages. They are blocks
of a hard chalk (not true clunch) which is rare
in Surrey (also found at Seale)

FOLLOW the track to the end of the row
and continue to the small brick bridge
ahead of you.

CROSS the bridge and follow the track
all the way to the end in the street.
In early spring it is attractive with golden
celandines (left top) and bright blue periwinkles
(right) but it is always pleasant as it skirts
round the back of the village and soon proves to
be surprisingly high above the water meadows of
the Wey valley down on your left.

TURN LEFT up the street towards the church.

A wide range of architecture makes the ramble worthwhile. Note the cottages with the upper floor projecting forwards, indicating that they are timber-framed
buildings under a protective coat of plaster. These
skirt you round to the space in front of the church
where the village stocks have been replaced.

The church with its copper spire looks good. It is
the work of Benjamin Ferrey who was particularly
successful at creating exteriors that are very
effective in their landscape setting. What would
Brockham green be without its church? Ferrey built that
too and in the same year as this one - 1846. With the
interiors he was less successful but this one is much
finer than Brockham's.

Aspects of its history are attractively displayed
inside where you'll find a memorial to the great
explorer of the N.W.Himalayas, Col. Haversham Godwin-
Austen, winner of the Founder's Medal of the Royal
Geographical Society. He was also an eminent geologist
as was his father, Robert Alfred Cloyne Godwin-Austen.

Among the incumbents described are William Oughtred
before he went on to Albury. He was a great man at
mathematics and taught Sir Christopher Wren, collected
the known maths of his day into a study
called 'Clavis Mathematicae' published in
1631 and is blessed or cursed by us all for
introducing the x multiplication sign.

Also at Shalford was David Railton who took
to the Dean of Westminster the idea for the
Tomb of the Unknown Warrior and the Union
Jack now hanging over it is said to have
been the pall used by Railton in France when
buring the dead during the war.

Shalford Mill
L. Houseman 1985.

ON LEAVING THE CHURCH RETURN DOWN THE STREET
LOOKING FOR THE NARROW LANE ON THE LEFT WHICH
IS SIGNPOSTED TO THE MILL (National Trust).

The walk down to the mill, past more old cottages and
views of gardens is always pleasant. The mill, over-
sailing the path was built in 1753 with brick for the
ground floor and timber-framing above, now protected
under tile-hanging on the front and weatherboarding on
the back. It is normally kept open at reasonable times,
when you are invited to go in and have a look. There
you will find the machinery complete which makes it a
great rarity in Surrey. It is of the 'low breastshot'
type and the bit to note is the spur wheel - hardly a
bit! It's a massive wooden wheel nine feet in diameter;
a masterpiece of carpentry.

In 1930 the secretary of the National Trust was mighty
startled to find a masked woman in front of her and
even more surprised to be presented with £100. It was
the first instalment towards the preservation of this

mill by the anonymous 'Ferguson's Gang'. This group was formed in 1927 by young people in their 20s who saw the real threat to our heritage by the post war building boom, as warned by architect Clough Williams-Ellis in his book 'England and the Octopus'. The Gang went on to raise money for subsequent projects and by the time the Second World War brought them to a halt they had raised some £4,500 for the National Trust. In 1989 the two surviving members presented a collage to the National Trust and revealed their identities.

Shalford Mill is reputed to be the setting for the illustration by Ernest Sheppard of Christopher Robin peering down into the water. The artist lived at Longdown on the hills behind, for part of his working life.

RETURN TO THE MAIN STREET and as you do so glance through to the left for a view of the Mill House with its 17th century brick work and Dutch gables.

TURN LEFT AND THEN CROSS THE ROAD TO TURN RIGHT UP DAGDEN ROAD if you wish to avoid walking along the main road.

This road appears to be a dead end but at the top TAKE THE FOOTPATH between the gardens. This will bring you on to the track by which you entered Shalford. TURN LEFT and retrace your steps down to the railway bridge and so back across the common to the starting point.

ALTERNATIVELY, instead of turning up Dagden Road continue along the main road, over the railway and so on to the common. The main A248 cuts off on the right to pass the Parrot and the starting point.

There is still a wide variety of architecture to be seen but nothing especially grand, although the old village school (now the First School) is far bigger than might be expected, except that there must have been a lot of children in all the workers' houses.

The most interesting building for many people will be the Methodist Church; non-conformists had a tough time in Surrey and the beginnings of formal communities were slow. Methodism is thought to have come to Guildford in 1829 and encouraged the surrounding villages to have meetings of their own. Shalford Methodists went to Pink's Hill for services and then in 1825 moved to the Chilworth Paper Mills until they were able to set up their own chapel here in 1843. It still stands. It is behind the present church which was registered for worship in 1895.

Another non-conformist story about the village is that the Puritan Baptist preacher and writer John Bunyan came here, that Vanity Fair in his 'Pilgrim's Progress' is based on Shalford Fair and so on. It's a good story but has been disproved. Evidently there is no break in the records concerning John Bunyan when he could have come here and there is certainly no reference that directly links the two - or so I am told!

Pussy Willow

MERROW DOWNS

Distance : 5 miles

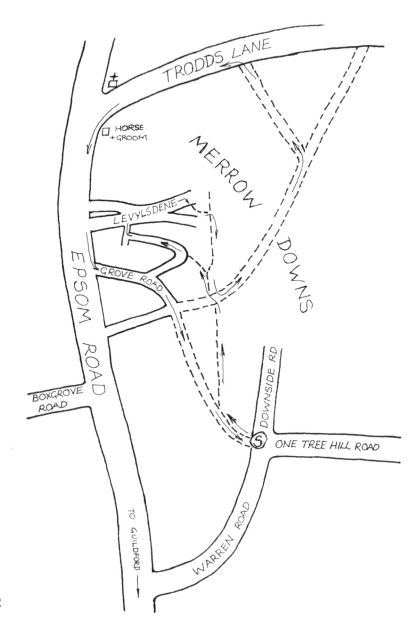

START (S on the map) at the junction
of Warren Road, Downside Road and
One Tree Hill... reached from
Guildford High Street by taking
Epsom Road by the Odeon Cinema,
going straight ahead at the
traffic lights and then first
right into Warren Road.

The starting point is at the edge
of the Downs where gardens and
street trees add interest;
(witch hazel illustrated right).

This high point affords wide
views out over Surrey to
the north. To help locate
places note the tall pale
modern block towering out
of the trees in the middle
distance and know that it is
the B.A.T. building in Woking
town centre.

Immediately before you are the open Downs which can be
a beautiful great swathe of golden grasses in high
summer. A number of paths entice ramblers out of the
road - take the right hand higher one which runs off
between two single trees in the distance. Note the
avenue of maples on the lower path.

FOLLOW THE PATH ACROSS THE DOWNS

At the end, PRESS AHEAD to the path that runs
beside the club house of Guildford Golf Club.

Do not skirt around the green but follow the
small path ahead to come out into LONGMEAD.

TURN RIGHT and walk downhill.

TURN RIGHT at the bottom into LEVYLSDENE

Walk uphill skirting the green.

After the foregoing wide open spaces, Levylsdene with its trees and houses appears quite suburban but it is, nevertheless, an historic and interesting spot.

Formerly called Levyl's Grove, it was here that the great Parliamentarian Arthur Onslow came to live on the death of his mother in 1715. The remains of his house, in flint and brick, can be found snuggled into the trees among the modern housing. It dates from the 17th and 18th centuries and looks rather incongruous amid the modernity - the grounds were divided up for redevelopment in 1955 which fortunately retained some of the fine trees which makes today's Levylsdene so distinctive. The important partnership of G.A.Jellicoe & Ptnrs. took a part, and theirs are the two houses next to the main road at the entrance.

Upon his marriage, Onslow moved to Imber or Ember Court at Thames Ditton. Thus he never lived in Clandon Park built by the family nearby, although some of his possessions are there. Upon his death he was buried at Thames Ditton but subsequently reinterred at Merrow churchyard although his memorial is in Holy Trinity, Guildford, adjacent to the Royal Grammar School he had attended as a child. His importance today lies in his instigation of the keeping of parliamentary records and of much of the procedure which Parliament still follows. (Clandon Park is a National Trust property open to the public).

At the top of LEVYLSDENE follow the surfaced path round to the RIGHT back to the edge of the golf course and there TURN RIGHT.

64

At the Club House, TURN LEFT on to another track.
(Or, if you've had enough - retrace route to start)

KEEP LEFT at the fork.

You will soon be among trees but best of all are the unexpected views from the Downs into the valleys and farms that make up the 'traditional' countryside that still slides up to Guildford in such an attractive way. Thank goodness there aren't miles of dreary suburbs!

Continue along this track, past Keeper's Cott. on the right. Although the road narrows through the woodland it is nevertheless clear.

When three trees appear as an isolated group in a clearing start looking out for a lesser track that runs off uphill to the left from a junction with other paths. FOLLOW THAT, up and over the hill and down to the road.

TURN LEFT at the road, enjoying its grassy flowery banks for ½mile or so and then the pavement begins, leading down to the church.

Many people ask us where the old race track was and so, if that is of interest, you can turn right instead of left when you reach the road and walk up to the end of the trees, on the edge of the golf course. At this point you are on the old track which crossed the road here. Golfers will be using part of it from the 6th to the 10th tee. The Golf Club was founded in 1886.

65

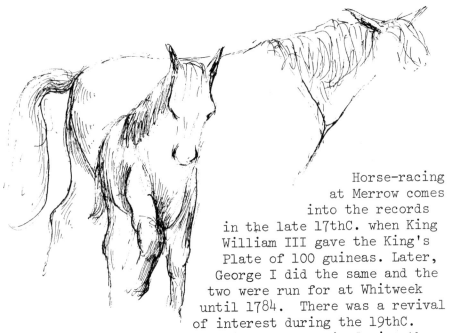

Horse-racing
at Merrow comes
into the records
in the late 17thC. when King
William III gave the King's
Plate of 100 guineas. Later,
George I did the same and the
two were run for at Whitweek
until 1784. There was a revival
of interest during the 19thC.
with the King's Plate becoming the Queen's during the
reign of Victoria but at the same time Epsom was more
popular and Ascot was founded so Merrow declined and
the last race was run in 1870. The grandstand (near
the present 10th hole) had been demolished some 20 yrs.
earlier.

(Our thanks to Guildford Golf Club for their
help and information on this topic.)

Walking down the hill to the church takes ramblers past
the timber-framed "Old Cottage", dating from the 16th/
17th centuries, which is a good reminder that you are
back in the heart of an ancient village.

The church on the right looks so very
Victorian and yet as soon as you
reach the north door you are under
the Norman chevron mouldings of
c.1150. Inside, the south arcade
is a little later, about 1200, still
with round arches but with matching
round capitals too. Otherwise most
of the church was rebuilt in 1842
by R.C.Hussey (his only work of
note to survive in Surrey?) and

then in 1881 the north
aisle was added by
Sir A.W.Blomfield
who did much work
in Surrey.

TURN LEFT at the bottom of the hill and leaving
the church behind you follow the main road to
The Horse and Groom.

The very name records the horse-racing days but only
since the 1880s. Before that it was called The Running
Horse, and before that it recorded a different sport
altogether, being called The Hare and Hounds. The
Onslow estates included 'The Warren' for hares, south

of Levylsdene. The date 1615 can
be found on the front of the pub
which no doubt began life as a
farmhouse but soon took advantage
of traffic on the main road to offer
accommodation to travellers bound
for Epsom Spa which began to develop
after 1618. The inn did well, judging
from the array of chimneys and large
windows; the hearth tax and the window
tax were still things of the future.

CONTINUE along the main road towards Guildford.
A few more old houses and cottages can be spotted but
most of the route is modern. The road itself became a
turnpike in 1758.

PASS the turning into Levylsdene and take the
NEXT LEFT into GROVE ROAD.

At the end, CONTINUE AHEAD and join the path
running through the avenue of maples which takes
you back over the downland landscape experienced at the
beginning of this ramble.

At the end of the path follow it round to the left
to find the starting point for the ramble.

67

TO ST. MARTHA'S HILL

Distance : 5½ miles approx.

Stepping off the street on to the grass presents an
expanse of hills and valleys, woods and fields, that
is such a surprise right next to Guildford. From the
Downs this ramble descends to the lowlands, up on to
St.Martha's Hill, down again and then back up on the
Downs at Pewley - often tiring but always rewarding.

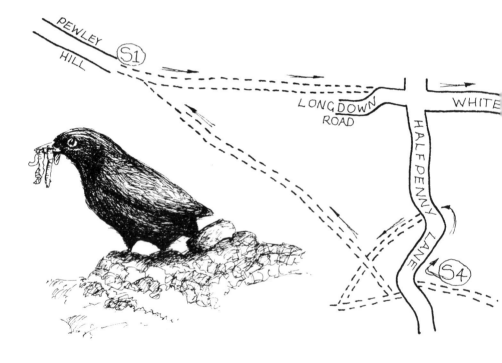

START -From GUILDFORD (S1), park at the top of Pewley
Hill (a very steep walk from the town), or, at the car
park for NEWLANDS CORNER (S2), or, either car park for
St.Martha's (S3 and S4).

DIRECTION as described, is clockwise to avoid the very
long steep climb up to Newlands Corner.

FROM GUILDFORD - PEWLEY HILL rises from the
junction of CASTLE STREET and SYDENHAM ROAD
beside the castle, behind TUNSGATE from the
HIGH STREET.

On the left near the top of Pewley Hill is a house
with a tower which was created in 1848 out of a former
Admiralty semaphore tower. It was part of a chain of
signalling stations built between London and Portsmouth
in 1821-2. Opposite is Pewley Fort, a companion to
Henley Fort on The Mount Ramble, built to defend London

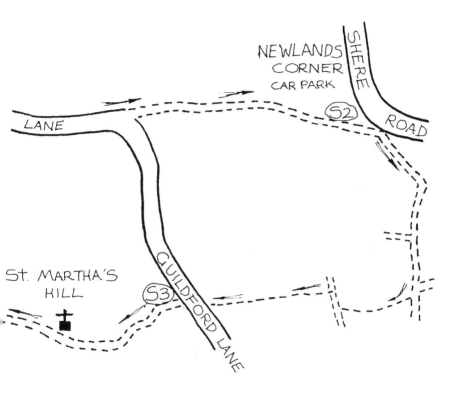

against possible invasion (c.1897-1905). This one is
different from the others in the chain for having such
extensive defences built around it.

AT THE TOP OF PEWLEY HILL WALK OUT ONTO THE
GRASSLAND

CONTINUE AHEAD ALONG THE TOP OF THE DOWNS, on
what is thought to be a particularly ancient trackway.
The grassland on either side is full of scented herbs,
glorious in high summer, from the lowly Thyme to the
taller mauve flowered Marjoram. There's purple Knapweed,
blue Scabious and multicoloured butterflies. Always there
are glorious views over to the right which will no doubt
lure you in that direction. That will not matter so long
as you keep in sight the hedge that runs along on your
left so that when another comes out at right angles from
it you can follow the track that cuts through the angle.

FOLLOW this track through the trees (said to have been
planted by gypsies) right to the end where it merges with
Longdown Road and follow that ahead to the crossroads.

You will pass the garden boundary of 'Long Meadow' on the
right which was completed in 1929 for the artist Ernest
Shepard, best known today for illustrating the books of
A.A.Milne but who was working for Punch at the time.

The house (which is NOT open to the public) does not
feature prominently in his autobiography even though he
lived here 30 years and remarried from here. It remains
much as he left it, from the wooden stair that angles up
from the garden to his first floor studio, to the garden
pond that is still recognisable from one of his pictures.
His oil painting now entitled "The View of Chantry Woods
from Long Meadow" does not show that view but the one
from the downland you have just
crossed. Inside the house is a
wonderful wooden staircase
created from a sketch he
made of one in a
Norfolk farmhouse.
To sit on there
certainly stirs
thoughts of
Christopher
Robin!

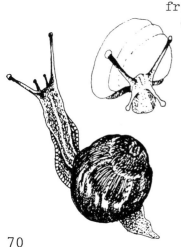

AT THE CROSSROADS cross over to continue ahead, along WHITE LANE. There's quite a variety of trees, wild flowers and birds all along here. In autumn look out for the bright orange seeds in the pods of the wild Gladden Iris (sketched below by Darren Hemsley).

Blackcap ♂

At the right hand BEND leave White Lane to continue ahead over the Downs.

Take the left path, all the way to the car park at Newlands Corner, if you want shade or wind protection.

Take the right hand path for the views and the great open spaces. This route takes you below the car park so cut up the bank if you need the toilets or refreshments.

From the car park go towards the entrance and take the track RIGHT which plunges off the Down through the trees.

If you have taken the lower path it will join with this track so simply turn right.

Once through the trees the route goes down over the chalk grassland again. Look out for juniper bushes: Surrey is one of the few counties where it still grows wild but even in Surrey it is far more scarce than it was a hundred years ago, so leave the berries to seed.

KEEP TO THIS TRACK

BEAR RIGHT AT THE PILL BOX

BEAR LEFT AT THE OLD CHALK PIT

IGNORE THE FARM ROAD TO THE RIGHT

TURN RIGHT on a path up the bank opposite the first track that goes off left.

TURN RIGHT after the horse pastures, onto a farm road.
FIRST LEFT very soon after and before the farm.

CROSS ROAD into CAR PARK FOR ST.MARTHA's (S3)

FOLLOW any track up to the top of the hill to the church, avoiding the areas fenced off for reclamation. The soil has changed completely. You are now off the chalk and on Folkestone Sand, coarse grained and far from fertile, so it's a heathland habitat, to which have been added foreign plants like laurel and Douglas fir.

St MARTHA's-on-THE-Hill, SURREY.   C. Howkins '68.

It is one of Surrey's most famous spots to visit, not just for the church in such a picturesque setting but for the views. These had become obscured by tree growth until the Great Storm of 1987 wiped out so many. Regular readers may be interested to know that the above illustration was the first by Chris Howkins ever publishe

St.Martha's Church was built originally by the Normans and became a possession of Newark Priory near Ripley until the Dissolution of the Monasteries in the 16thC. Then it went into private ownership with the land and fell into ruins until the architect Henry Woodyer was given the job of rebuilding it in 1848. He used as much of the original as was sound and added new material in the style of 1170, including one great change from the original design - he gave it a central tower and what a masterful addition that is too.

This much-loved church is open to the public during the summer. The interior is a simple one, in keeping with its Norman beginning but with some Victorian designs, like the east window. There is a memorial to John St Loe Strachy (not buried here) who built the big house at Newlands Corner. He was editor of The Spectator. Outside, next to the eastern churchyard gate is a stone memorial to the musician and actress Yvonne Arnaud, whose ashes were scattered on the hill in 1958. It is a famous hill, thought to have been a lasting Christian retreat after the Romans departed; one of only perhaps two such places in Surrey.

Common
Toad

LEAVE by the western gate to continue the ramble down the hill.

The Great Storm opened up the views and still there is a great deal of timber lying on the hill. most of it is now encrusted with the wavy edged bracket fruits of a fungus. This is the one that causes 'heart rot' and so we can see all too clearly how heavily infected the trees were, and therefore doomed to an early death, long before the storm. Most trees are infected in this way. What looks like a healthy tree to us is fighting off biological attacks, just as our own immune systems are fully at work at all times. It is all a matter of time!

At the bottom TURN RIGHT down the lane.

There are other ways but we like this route because of the chance at the bottom to peep over into a pond on the right to see if there is anything of note. If there is ever anything exciting here we have always missed it! The fun is in the looking.

As you go down the lane take the FIRST
BRIDLEWAY LEFT

In dry weather this route is deep in loose
sand which will slow you down - and finish
off the weary!

BEAR RIGHT AT THE JUNCTION
and take the long straight
route back across the flank
of the Downs to the
starting point of the
ramble.

When the wind is blowing
rain in your face this
becomes a hideous trek
but on a fine sunny day
in summer it is very
pleasant and if you come
when the season's first
crop of butterflies is
fresh on the wing then it
is very pleasant indeed.

For those ramblers who
would prefer a longer
ramble through this
countryside there is
the option of adding on
the next ramble to extend
the route eastwards to
take in the Silent Pool.

Right - the fruits of the rowan
or mountain ash. This, with the
elder and the hawthorn are the three
most magical trees in Surrey. From
the folklore collected so far this one
would seem to have the most superstitions
associated with it.

SILENT POOL AND ALBURY DOWNS
Distance: 3 miles approx.

This ramble can be added on to the previous
one (compare maps for linking up) or simply
enjoyed in its own right.

START: (S1) Newlands Corner Car Park
             signposted off A25 at top of hill.
       (S2) Silent Pool Car Park
             signposted off A25 dual carriageway.

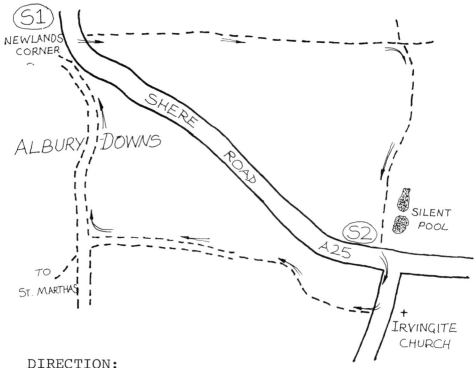

DIRECTION:
The circuit is described in
clockwise direction as the climb up
the downs to Newlands Corner is not quite as demanding
as the longer climb up from the Silent Pool.

From Newlands Corner
Car Park walk back
to the entrance
and CROSS OVER
the main road.

At quiet times a variety
of birds come down into the
car park to see what food the
visitors have left behind and
some, (like the Turtle Dove shown
right) come down to pick up grit
which they need in their digestive
systems.

CONTINUE along the path marked North
Downs Way, along the crest of the hill.

This section of the ramble is easy going
because of it being along the top of the
Downs and it is also very rewarding as
gaps between the trees yield more
expansive views out over southern
Surrey and out across West Sussex
to the distant blue line of the
South Downs.

The sheltering trees provide an
attractive habitat for a wide
range of creatures. The one
that is probably going to draw
attention to itself is the Grey
Squirrel scrabbling noisily in
the fallen leaves. On the cold
winter's morning when this was
prepared one was disturbed, not
by us, but by a trio of Roe
Deer.

TURN RIGHT at the cross-
paths and plunge steeply
over the downland scarp
through young woodland.

KEEP LEFT at
the bottom and
leave the fields
by the gate ahead,
into a trackway and note
the signs for the Silent Pool.

The Silent Pool has become a popular spot to visit
since a local writer in Victorian times featured it in
a Romantic novel, involving a visit by King John. It
was of course presented as fact but research has shown
that the writer, Martin Tupper of Albury, did not work
from local legend but created one! Many people are
now convinced that there is a connection between the
Silent Pool and King John – it's a good story – but
not a true one.

The signs will lead to the Silent Pool and its
companion pool which can be explored at will
before returning to the trackway to continue
on ahead.

Lighting and season will probably play a large part in
the amount of pleasure gained from a visit to the pools.
A soft light on early spring greens with reflections in
the water will earn a page of the memory book and so
will some of the autumnal days when the year is good
for colour. Sometimes it's a matter of looking upwards,
when the pool is in shadow but a low sun is catching
the tree tops around it. Maybe watching a moorhen
tip-toeing through the mud will be enough.

WARNING - The main road is ahead. Take care
with children and dogs.

CROSS THE ROAD to take the road opposite
for Albury.

LOOK FOR, AND USE, THE STILE IN
THE HEDGE ON THE RIGHT HAND SIDE.

WALK AHEAD from the stile,
keeping the fence on your
right side.
You have now come
down into the
beautiful valley
of the little
Tillingbourne.
With the Downs
running along on
your right and
the Leith Hill
range on the left
it is difficult to
believe that within
walking distance is
the town centre of Guildford.

CROSS THE NEXT TWO STILES

Look back from time to time for attractive
views of the tower of the Catholic Apostolic
Church among the trees at Albury. This may
look at first sight to be medieval Perpendicular
architecture but only came into being in the 1840s at
the expense of the banker Henry Drummond who had moved
into Albury Park. He became deeply involved with the
Irvingite Movement with its Roman Catholic tendencies,
making Albury the centre of its activities which did not
go down too well with the local Anglican church! He did,
however, build them a new parish church but that's all
part of a long but fascinating story best left for winter
reading.

With so much
agricultural
land having to
be taken out of
traditional usage
the character of this
landscape may change.
Private lands like the
Albury and Shere Estates
are working to preserve
much of the scenery and
responding to calls for greater
public access. Without their
help such traditional working
habitats as the oakwoods with hazel
coppice beneath (illustrated) will be even more
severely threatened. The Hazel is already our most
threatened tree as the grey squirrels strip the nuts
preventing the growth of new trees to replace the old.

THE SECOND STILE puts you into a track which
you FOLLOW. It cuts across the entrance to a
quarry so take care and NOTE THE WARNING SIGNS.

80

PASS the first house,
(Timbers Croft) and
KEEP LEFT.

PASS two cottages
after which TURN RIGHT
and walk UPHILL.

KEEP RIGHT at the clearing and
take a deep breath for a steep
climb.

The steepness gives a good excuse,
if you need one, for going slowly
and seeing what is about. The pheasant
(cock illustrated) is still a game bird to be found in
the Tillingbourne Valley. Once they were bred every
year in their thousands on the local estates for the
winter sport of shooting them.

AT JUNCTION FOLLOW ROUND TO THE LEFT and this
track will lead, very steeply, back to the
starting point (S1) at Newlands Corner.

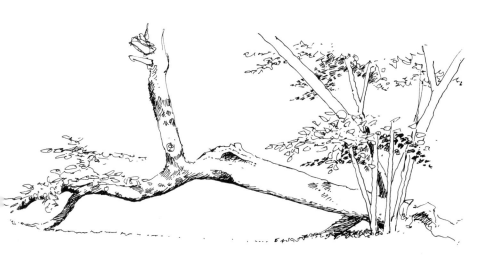

FROM STOKE BRIDGE:

Stoke Lock : 3/4 mile ret.
Bowers Lock: 2 3/4 miles ret.
Triggs Lock : 6 3/4 miles ret.

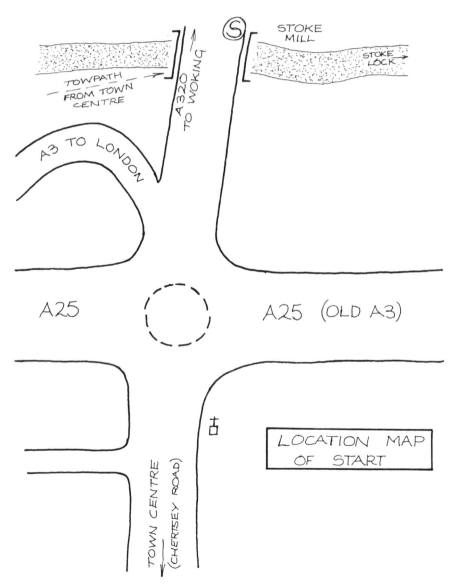

LOCATION MAP OF START

THE RAMBLE explores the Wey Valley downstream of the town centre, where it soon becomes green meadowland again and has historic interest.

UNFORTUNATELY there is no circular route that we feel is sufficiently attractive to recommend but suggestions are given in the text.

START : AT STOKE BRIDGE over the River Wey, carrying the A320 north of the Guildford By-pass, to Woking.

TO REACH THE START

    ON FOOT (1) By Towpath, following it all the way downstream from the town bridge.

           (2) By taking Chertsey Street out of North Street (earlier ramble) and following that all the way to the By-pass and beyond. It changes its name to Stoke Road.

   BY CAR as per option (2) above is simplest. Find street parking near the bridge.

Stoke Bridge is only a convenient starting place and is not of interest in itself (built by Surrey County Council in 1926) but upstream stands the Rowbarge pub. It is one of the very few commemorations of the old days of barge traffic on the waterway but more importantly, it stands approximately on the site of Sir Richard Weston's first modification of the river before it was made navigable.

From here he had cut an artificial channel for some three miles over his land to link both sides of a loop in the river. He installed a lock to control levels, so that he could deliberately flood his meadows to irrigate them during droughts and to help keep the frost off in late spring when his cattle were in desperate need of fresh grass. There was no winter feed for cattle in those days, except hay, until Sir Richard introduced turnips. Work began here in 1618; the first half mile was later used as the course of the Wey Navigation and the abandoned section has been lost. Only slight signs remain on the ground today although it can be traced on old maps.

RAMBLERS arriving from Guildford Town Centre by way of the towpath will approach through the meadows towards the bridge and the view illustrated opposite.

From the bridge join the towpath on the downstream side to follow it out through meadowland scenery to Stoke Lock. On the right, at the beginning, is the Stoke Mill complex.

Sir Richard Weston built the first mill here in 1635, so far as is known today. The site continued milling corn until 1956 but over the generations other activities have employed the water power, often simultaneously :- sawing timber, processing flax (lin) into linseed oil and its products, and paper-making which ended in 1869. They have all been important Surrey industries.

The oldest building on the site today is probably the mill house which claims to date from 1650 although what we see is all Victorian. The mill building is of 1879 and was built of brick to reduce fire risk. A three storey timber mill had been gutted in 1863. Its successor was part brick but still weatherboarded. That was replaced with this impressive version, rising six storeys as an imposing monument to Victorian enterprise. It was the case of 'get big' and join the new factory system or go out of business, as did so many of the little Surrey mills. Three new versions were built in the Wey Valley - Ockham, Coxes Lock and this, the grandest of all.

Care was taken to avoid ugly flat surfaces of red brick, with architectural relief and the decorative use of yellow brick. In 1988 there was a threat of demolition which roused local affections and so it has been preserved, converted to office use.

CONTINUE along the towpath, downstream from the mill site.

It is an attractive walk down to the lock and its cottage. One of the sights you will not be able to see is the one sketched below, from on board the horse drawn narrowboat in 1989 when The National Trust celebrated 25 years of caring for the Wey Navigation. Special permission was granted to them to re-enact the days of old but as this entailed having the police stop all the traffic on the by-pass to allow the horse to cross it is not likely to be repeated in a hurry!

Stoke Lock is the oldest lock on the waterway and was
the first such lock to be built in Surrey. Dating from
1619-20 it was built by Sir Richard Weston as part of
his initial scheme to alter the River Wey to benefit
his Sutton Place estates here. He is said to have
brought back the idea of pound locks from his travels
in the Low Countries. This may well be true but he was
not the first person to use them in England judging
from the records pertaining to earlier river improvement
schemes elsewhere, which imply the use of pound locks.
The notion that they were a Dutch invention has been
disproved by archaeologists working in Italy. Much of
Sir Richard's work at agricultural improvement was,
however, pioneering work.

The style of the lock cottage is not really a Guildford
style. Such buildings are found further south around
Haslemere.

Ramblers will find this an attractive spot to visit, with views out round the loop in the river. When the weather is kind it is a good place to loiter and watch the river craft using the lock.

For those who wish to ramble further it is worthwhile to continue down the towpath to the next lock (about one mile).

For those who wish to return to Stoke Bridge but by a different route there is the option of leaving Stoke Lock by its access road and continuing along the highway to a turning left into Old Farm Road. At the end turn left again along the A320 to the bridge. This is not very attractive but neither is it ruined by heavy traffic etc.

This text continues to describe the towpath for those who wish to continue rambling on.

CONTINUE down the
towpath.

Look out for kestrels.
The mature trees offer
suitable nest sites
while the meadows
provide suitable
hunting grounds.
They also go over
to the A3 to seek
small rodents in
the grass verges.
The ramble down
through here has
the widest range of
birds of any of the rambles in this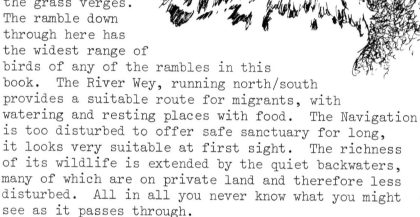
book. The River Wey, running north/south
provides a suitable route for migrants, with
watering and resting places with food. The Navigation
is too disturbed to offer safe sanctuary for long,
it looks very suitable at first sight. The richness
of its wildlife is extended by the quiet backwaters,
many of which are on private land and therefore less
disturbed. All in all you never know what you might
see as it passes through.

Along here can be found birds like the Coot; common
wherever there is a good expanse of water but rather
wary of the narrow confines of waterways like this.
Here they frequent an old loop of the river, on the
far side, which was not cut through by Sir Richard
Weston but in the 1930s as part of the River Wey
Improvement Scheme.

Wild flowers of wet meadows can be found too, right up
to the towpath. Thus it is possible to enjoy some at
close quarters without getting wet feet! Not only is
the wildlife under the protection of the National Trust
but some of the adjoining land here comprises part of
Guildford Council's Riverside Park.

Pollarded willows, so much part of people's notion
of an English riverside scene, are now scarce in
Surrey. These are maintained by the National Trust.
There were once beds of osiers at many points along
the waterway which, it is presumed, supplied extra
material for the willow basket industry of the North
Surrey/Thames-side area. It was one of the five
main basket centres in the country.

90

At the sharp bend to the right, excess water flows out
to follow the old course of the river. It meanders off
into a great loop that is reunited with the Navigation
not very far ahead. During its course it
has cut a bluff into the rise of the
land and up on there was the great
house of Sutton Place where Sir
Richard lived. Indeed it still
stands but at the time of
writing was not open
to the public.

Wild white violets
grow along here.
Look for them in
April.

Soon after the right
hand bend an old iron
bridge comes into view.
This used to carry the lane
from Burpham to Jacobs Well
but it now leads nowhere,
since the modern bridge was
built a little further downstream. For generations there
was a wooden bridge here,
until Surrey County Council
took over responsibility for
it in 1934 and built this iron
one which now belongs to the
National Trust. It is known as Bowers Bridge.

Just beyond Bowers Bridge is Bowers Mill and Bowers
Lock; it is worth going that far before turning back.
There is nothing to see of the mill - first recorded
in 1733, it ceased work by 1910, fell into disrepair
and was demolished in 1945. For most of its working
life it was a corn mill but in early days it was a
paper-making mill at the same time, and, for a short
spell was an oil mill working linseed oil. The present
house on the site was originally the laundry for Sutton
Place. The sluices were put in during the 1930s as

part of the River Wey Improvement Scheme. It was most
likely that it was at that time that the watercourses
for the mill were removed.

This is not a disappointing spot though. There's a
grand old oak by the towpath that looks as though it
was there in Sir Richard's time. Then from the lock
there's an attractive route round to the lower level
which is necessary because here the river loop described
previously rejoins the Navigation.

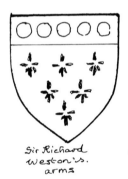

Sir Richard
Weston's.
arms

There is a good view out from under
the trees across wide meadowland,
although saplings have been planted
so this view will soon change and
become enclosed.

The land is the Sutton Place estate
and is kept strictly private. You
can, however, walk the towpath at
the invitation of the National Trust.

To walk on to the next lock is a
further two miles (described
after the next option).

        To turnabout and retrace the route to
    Stoke Bridge is nearly 1½ miles but if
you walked out from Guildford town centre there
is an alternative route back from Bowers Bridge
to the top of Guildford High Street:-

This alternative route is mainly through the
residential areas, with some houses of minor
interest, plenty of trees and some gardens with
interesting or pleasing plants. If you come
from an urban area you will probably like it
but if you have come from the country you will
probably prefer the towpath.

The route is simple:- take the residential
road from Bowers Bridge and follow it round to
the left and up onto the new road and turn
right (deviate left, just to view the scene from the
new bridge if you wish) and take first right into

Burpham Lane and follow this
village street right round to
the roundabout at the top.

The church is by Henry Woodyer,
one of the under-rated Victorian
architects who did a lot of his
work in Surrey. This chapel-of-
ease dates from 1859 and has been
kept simple as indeed must have
been the rural hamlet of Burpham
in those days.

The street has one or two houses
of some age that will catch the
eye but it is more rewarding to
note the gardens (Aubrieta and
Iris pumila illustrated).

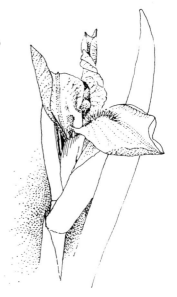

At the roundabout turn right
and follow the main road
to the next roundabout.
This used to be the busy
A3 but is now the quieter
A3100 now that the new A3
has been built. Even so,
it can be busy during the
rush hours. There are
shops and a pub at the
start.

At the next roundabout
cross over to continue
ahead along London Road
for the town centre.
This will join the top
of the High Street.

The first part is alongside
Stoke Park where the grass
will no doubt make a welcome
change from the pavements!
Good views across to the
Cathedral and University.

93

Returning to the option of continuing along the towpath from Bowers Lock for a further two miles to Triggs Lock, this is only for those who do not mind the walk back, or, can arrange for someone with a car to collect them at the far end.

The option of being met at Send church is not recommended unless it is a drought summer as the footpath across the meadows is so often waterlogged. It is better to be met at the top of the access road to Triggs Lock:-

Using the Street Atlas, follow the A320 from Stoke Bridge towards Woking but turn right at the roundabout at Jacobs Well, into Clay Lane. Take first left up Blanchards Hill and first right along Sutton Green Road until the road bears left and a farm track continues ahead. Meet there.

The walk down to Triggs Lock is one of simple pleasures through meadowland and woodland with views across to Send church.

After the first great field (Cooper's Meadow) another 1930s channel takes excess water away into the old river which cuts out on the corner ahead to meander through the fields at Send before rejoining with the Navigation at the next lock point. Between these two outlets Broadoak Bridge carries the driveway of Sutton Place over the waters. There is no exit here.

Under the bridge is a roller (and supports for two more) which used to guide the towropes through without chafing on the brickwork. There's another on the next bend. The weir there is part of the original layout of the Navigation, which now runs straight up to another right angled bend (Pipper's Point or Whippet's Turn) before running off through trees and fields.

The moored boats indicate that the lock is just ahead; canal enthusiasts might like to know that it has "an unusual arrangement of paddles". With these the water level was controlled until the National Trust built the tumbling bay to remove any excess.

The little cottage (illustrated overleaf) was built about 1820 and restored by The National Trust in 1987. In former days this was where the barge people brought their washing to be done by the lock keeper's wife.

This is a very attractive spot with which to end the book.